Benjamin Zephaniah

A PROFILE

Verna Wilkins

Tamarind Ltd

OTHER BOOKS IN

Black Profiles Series

LORD JOHN TAYLOR OF WARWICK
DR. SAMANTHA TROSS
MALORIE BLACKMAN
BARONESS PATRICIA SCOTLAND
MR JIM BRAITHWAITE

Acknowledgements

from *Talking Turkeys* by Benjamin Zephaniah (Viking, 1994)
© Benjamin Zephaniah, 1994

Pages 10-11, extract (20 lines, p 38)
    from 'A Day in the Life of Danny the Cat'
Page 17, 'Think me' (p 70, 11 lines)
Page 28, 'Who's Who' (p 48, 7 lines)
Pages 42-44, 'Body Talk' (pp 14-15, 48 lines)
Page 35, extract (4 lines, p 89) from 'Talking Turkeys'

Published by Tamarind Ltd 1999
P O Box 52
Northwood, Middlesex HA6 1UN,
England

Text © Verna Wilkins
Illustrations © Gillian Hunt

ISBN 1-870516-38-9

Printed in Singapore

Contents

Benjamin Zephaniah received an honorary doctorate from the University of North London on 3 December 1998 for his achievements as a poet and playright, and particularly for his contribution to the literary community and his humanitarian work.

CHAPTER ONE

The Early Years

BENJAMIN OBADIAH IQBAL ZEPHANIAH was born in Birmingham, on a crisp, cold March morning, in 1958. A few minutes later, his sister followed him into the world, screaming. Benjamin was the quiet twin.

Benjamin's family was poor. Their home in Birmingham had two rooms downstairs and two upstairs. On freezing winter mornings, when the frost made beautiful, cracked ice patterns on the

inside of his narrow window, Benjamin had to go out of the front door, around the side of the house and into the yard to get to the toilet. Each toilet door had the house number stuck high above the latch.

The houses stood flat-faced and weary, and the street ran right in front of the row of shabby front doors. There were a few trees, some bent and some broken, scattered on patches of earth battered bald by football and cricket. The Zephaniahs were the only black family in the neighbourhood, and Benjamin and his twin sister were the only black pupils in their school.

CHAPTER TWO

Under Attack

WHEN HE WAS ABOUT EIGHT YEARS OLD, Benjamin's parents were having one of their many arguments. He ducked out of the house and escaped into the street. Some marbles dropped out of a small hole in his pocket. As he crouched down to pick them up, he heard his sister scream.

"Watch out Benj!"

Benjamin shot upright, and saw a cyclist, riding straight at him, one arm in the air. With a blinding thud, a brick struck him smack in the face. The hooligan rode off still laughing. With blood pouring from a painful gash, Benjamin ran back to his house.

"Lord have mercy," cried his mother, as she hugged him.

His parents had to stop fighting to take him to the hospital. The wound was to leave a life-long scar.

A few weeks later a Pakistani family moved into the street. From that day, the hooligans targeted them instead. Although Benjamin felt sorry for their children, he was grateful to be left alone.

CHAPTER THREE
Family Split

BY THE TIME BENJAMIN WAS NINE, his parents had another set of twins and four more children. The house was crowded and his parents were still quarrelling. Benjamin hated this and often stood between them.

After the zillionth argument, when his father had stormed out to go to work, Benjamin's mother called him to one side.

"Come here Benji, love," she whispered, "get your things together. We're leaving."

"Why?" asked Benjamin. "What about the others? We can't leave them."

"It's just you and me he hurts. Your dad loves the others. He can manage. Quick, let's go," his mother replied.

Benjamin stopped asking questions and stuffed some clothes into a bag. His mother took his hand and quietly they slipped out of the house.

They travelled by bus for a while. Then they walked for miles. Again and again Benjamin stood on the pavement, while his mother knocked on every door.

"Have you got a room for me and the boy to rent?" she pleaded.

Time after time heads shook and doors were shut in their faces.

Just when Benjamin's feet were beginning to hurt badly, a kind Pakistani family agreed to rent them a room in their house.

"I'm going to get us some food, Benji," his mother called to him from the door.

Benjamin turned to look, but he was too tired to speak. By the time she had walked out of the rickety front gate, Benjamin had collapsed onto the narrow, lumpy bed and was soon fast asleep.

A New School and No Friends

"WAKE UP BOY, WAKE UP. We have to find you a school. Come on, come on."

"Is it morning already?" Benjamin groaned and covered his head.

The new school was awful. He felt lost. Everyone had their gang sorted.

"How did you get on today?" his mother asked as soon as he poked his head round the door that evening.

"Same as usual, Ma. Schools are all alike. Boring," muttered Benjamin.

"Don't say that Benji love. It might seem boring now, but try and learn as much as you can in school. It'll help you get a good job later on."

Every weekday morning Benjamin left the house at the same time. Most evenings his mother asked him about school, always the same question.

"How did you get on today?"

Sometimes Benjamin replied. Sometimes he said nothing. He didn't have anything to tell her.

After a few weeks his mother sat him down for a serious talk.

"Benjamin," she asked, "exactly what do you do in school all day long?"

"I make up poems," said Benjamin.

He couldn't tell her that he spent ages hidden in the playground, watching the animals in the next-door farm. He couldn't tell her his only friend was the farm cat.

"Where are these poems then?" his mum quizzed him.

"In my head," he answered "with all the rest, OK!"

"Will you tell me one?' his mother asked gently.

Benjamin had never told anyone about his poems before and he was nervous. He gave a little cough and then began.

"It's about a cat," he explained by way of an introduction. "A cat I've been watching and making friends with."

Danny wakes up
Checks for mice
Checks for birds

Checks for dogs
Checks for food

Finds a private place in the garden
Eats
And sleeps.

Danny has hobbies
Being stroked
Car watching
And smelling feet

He loves life
Keeps fit
And keeps clean
Every night he covers himself
In spit
Then he eats
And sleeps.

"That's brilliant Benji. It's poetry!" said his mother, pulling him onto her lap and giving him a big hug. "I wish I could do that."

"Do what, cover yourself in spit?" giggled Benjamin.

"Hey, watch it!" said his mother, and they both burst out laughing.

CHAPTER FIVE

On the Move Again

HE'D ONLY BEEN AT THE SCHOOL FOR six miserable weeks when his father tracked them down. His mother swiftly moved them to another address.

"Not another school, Ma," moaned Benjamin.

"You have to go. You have to make something of yourself, boy. You have to learn!"

"Ma," pleaded Benjamin. "I'm not learning."

"Don't be silly, Benji. You're a clever little lad. You'll be all right. Wait and see."

"Have you made friends Benjamin?" his mother asked sometime later.

"Yeah, lots," he muttered.

He couldn't tell his mother that because they moved so much, it was hard to make friends. He made friends with cats and birds and small animals like ants, whenever and wherever he sat down on his own.

"How can I go on eating meat when animals are my only friends," he pondered one day. Benjamin decided to become a vegetarian.

Suddenly, it seemed for no reason at all, they moved again. And again.

They moved from Birmingham to Manchester, then to Worcestershire. So many rooms and so many schools, that he simply lost count, although he was brilliant at counting. But he just could not read. He never stayed long enough in one place to learn how.

At last he found a school that was bearable. His teachers found that he excelled at all kinds of sports.

They also learned that he could draw and paint. It was *how* this came to light, that was the problem. He'd signed his work. And he'd used the playground wall as his canvas!

Benjamin was suspended immediately.

CHAPTER SIX

Loneliness Leads to Trouble

"WHAT AM I GOING TO DO!" Benjamin asked himself sitting in his one-roomed home, on a grey Monday. Looking at the same things over and over again was easily the worst thing in the world.

Benjamin missed his twin sister. "I wonder if she misses me," he whispered to himself.

He missed her and it made him a bit sad, so he made up a poem in his head for her.

Think Me
I want to be
In someone's mind
For ever
And ever
All right

I want my picture taken
I must be someone's thought
Somebody somewhere
Dream of me
I want to be Remembered
Remembered

Then he walked out of the house. He stopped outside Burger Brunch in the town centre at about 10.30am. He thought his luck had changed because by 11 o'clock he'd made three new friends – Justin, Curtis and Shaun.

"We're the Champs," grinned Justin.

"Yeah," chorused Curtis and Shaun.

"You got chucked out too?" asked Justin

"Yeah, from St Martin's," said Benjamin. He hunched his shoulders as they did, to look hard.

"We're from Bush Lane. Doing bags today. Wanna join up?"

"Yeah, if you like." Benjamin dug his hands into his pockets and slouched along with them. They hadn't gone far when a woman with a red bag came along. Benjamin kept walking.

"**RUN!**" suddenly blasted into his ear. It happened so quickly that Benjamin missed the action. He ran. The police caught them within minutes. Justin was so scared, he hadn't even let go of the bright red plastic handbag.

CHAPTER SEVEN

A Tussle with the Law

GOING TO COURT WAS FRIGHTENING and horrid. He kept shivering, even though it wasn't that cold. The sleeves on his borrowed jacket were much too short. "I feel silly in this," he muttered, tugging at the collar.

"Quiet!" came the loudest whisper he'd ever heard.

He felt even more silly, because he didn't have a clue what was going on. All the comings and goings. Bowing and scraping. Strange wigs and robes. It didn't feel real! But there was his mother. She was real. She was crying.

"What's going to happen to you, Benjamin?" she sobbed. He was truly sorry. He'd never meant to hurt his Mum, or anyone else. But he just wished she'd stop embarrassing him. He curled up his toes in his shoes and groaned.

When the session in court ended, he was sent to an approved school.

"Approved by whom?" Benjamin wondered.

The place was terrible. Woodwork classes weren't too bad. Games were okay. On weekdays, two teachers visited. Scarcely anyone there could read.

"We're not touching *them!*" said Benjamin's mate, pointing to the picture books for young children the teacher was holding. Others made gagging noises.

The teachers didn't bother to set homework. Benjamin didn't mind. The boys gave each other lessons. They learned how to pick pockets, open safes, fight and put people down.

CHAPTER EIGHT
A Captive Audience

ONE REALLY BORING, WET MORNING, Benjamin found an engine that one of the older boys had taken apart. He spent three days putting it back together again. It worked beautifully.

"Who showed you how to fix that?" asked his supervisor.

"Nobody," answered Benjamin. "I worked it out! Wasn't that difficult."

"Smart wotsit," muttered the supervisor.

Later, Benjamin heard the supervisor talking to his mates. "That Zephaniah boy, he's clever. Sharp brain he's got," he told them. "We've got to watch him. He could be difficult!"

Benjamin liked the gardener. He was a good bloke. He used the engine Benjamin had fixed to power the pump in the vegetable garden. For the first time since he could remember, Benjamin felt that he'd done something right. He'd enjoyed working on that engine and was glad it was being used.

One night, when there was nothing on the telly, and the boys were sick of snooker, Benjamin performed poems for them. They had a fantastic time. Soon Benjamin was on the table, rapping out poems while the other boys drummed on the floor and on the tables and chairs. The staff let

the boys get on with it. One peered in and even asked if he could join them.

He looked silly in his suit, as he nodded his head up and down. He tapped his foot to the rhythm but he was out of time and out of place. Benjamin couldn't decide what the boys enjoyed more. His poems or the supervisor joining in.

CHAPTER NINE

Off to Jamaica

JUST BEFORE BENJAMIN WAS RELEASED from the approved school, his mother had an idea. She knew that Benjamin was really bright. She just knew from the way he remembered things. She knew from the way he asked questions. Questions that had answers that he seemed too young to understand. Questions that she didn't even know the answers to.

"Tell you what," she said to Benjamin one day. "Go see your grandmother in Jamaica. It'll do you the world of good. She is a wise woman. Don't worry about how old she is, just go."

In Jamaica, Benjamin had a wonderful time. His grandmother's house was always busy. And she cooked his favourite food, just the way he liked it. Her ackee was good. Her callalloo was better. Best of all was her butter bean stew. He loved it.

"Fe you, darlin' chile," she'd say, smiling, as she served up another large plate of food.

Aunts, uncles and cousins came and went. They stopped for a chat and often for a meal. He made many, many friends. The weather was great and the sunsets were spectacular. He loved the music and

the rhythm of the voices around him. Poetry flowed through his head all the time.

He liked twilight time best, when the men gathered under a large tree to play dominoes. He recited poems to them sometimes. They joked about his strange accent, but shouted "Encore – again, again!" It was good.

But even better, the teachers were black. So were the police and the priests, mostly everybody. Benjamin felt comfortable there. He stayed six months with his grandmother. He felt better than he had done in all his years in England. But everyone his age who he met in Jamaica could read and write brilliantly. Embarrassed, he kept away from schools.

CHAPTER TEN

Home Again

BACK IN ENGLAND, HIS MOTHER HUGGED HIM.

"Come with me to church Benji?" she asked.

"Church, what for?" asked Benjamin. "Only little children and old people go to church, Mum, I'm fourteen years old."

"Just come, right? This minister," she said, "he has a way with words. They just hold you."

The following Sunday, Benjamin ambled up the steps of the Triumphant Church of God.

Hell-fire and brimstone preaching boomed around the church. It meant nothing to him.

But when the minister read the gospel, Benjamin whispered, "Good lyrics." His mother smiled.

Back home, he was able to repeat great chunks of what the minister had read. His mother was delighted. Benjamin asked her to read him all the names of the books of the Bible. Then he repeated them, with snapping fingers and swaying hips, from Genesis right to the end. And in the right order.

"You're a genius, Benji, boy," said his mother.

Benjamin just smiled.

That Christmas, he performed at the Community

Hall. He swayed his way through the bits of the Bible that he'd learned off by heart from church and from his mother.

Some of the older people thought he was irreverent. But by the end of his performance, he had the whole audience praising the Lord and clapping. Benjamin was in seventh heaven.

"YESSSS!" he rejoiced. "I can do this," he thought. "And I like it, I love it. I'm a poet."

When he arrived home he made up a poem about being a poet.

I used to think Nurses
Were Women
I used to think Police
Were Men
I used to think poets
Were boring
Until I became
    one of Them.

CHAPTER ELEVEN

Jail

HE WAS A PERFORMER. He knew it. He just did. But he couldn't read or write. Not properly.

"How can I succeed when reading and writing are so important and I can't do any of it?" he thought to himself.

No schools would have him so he drifted back into trouble. The years went by, and Benjamin

couldn't see any way out. The police were always stopping him and questioning him for no reason.

"It's the hair, Benjamin," his mother told him.

"It's mine," replied Benjamin, "I didn't steal it!"

"You know what I mean!" said his mother.

"Yes, I know Mum, but it's right for me."

Then just after his 21st birthday, he was involved in one awful fight. Benjamin was put into prison. He was desperately unhappy.

Day after day, he asked himself, "How can I make sense of my life stuck behind locked doors?"

It was there, when he had all the time in the world to think, he realised how angry he was. He was angry with his father. He was angry with the police. He was angry with the whole world.

Throughout this time, his mother stood by him. She'd travel hundreds of miles for a short visit. Sometimes, she arrived worn out and wistful.

"How're you holding up Benji, love?" she would ask smiling. But now it was a bone-tired smile and her eyes were damp.

"Not too bad, y'know, Mum," he'd reply. But, Benjamin felt horrible. He was causing her pain.

His mother's regular visits were one thing that helped him to make it through his worst times. The other was that he made up endless poems and stored them in his head.

In that dreadful hole of a prison, he made a big decision. "I must get a grip on this word thing," he promised himself. "This reading, this writing."

At last the day came when he was let out of prison.

"No matter what," he muttered as he turned away from the stark, ugly building. "I'm never going back inside. Never, never. Animals shouldn't be in cages, and humans neither. I'll never do anything, anything to allow anyone, anyone, to put me back in there."

And Benjamin cried openly as his mother walked up
the hill towards him.

CHAPTER TWELVE

A New Beginning

TWO WEEKS LATER, HE ENROLLED IN an Adult Education Class. He paid £1 per lesson and before long, he'd done it. He was on his way.

"I'm a writer! I'm a poet!" Benjamin would say to anyone who cared to listen.

"You're a criminal," they answered with their eyes, as they looked at him sideways.

Benjamin couldn't find work. Wandering around on some wasteland one day, he found pieces of discarded wood. He made rough and ready carvings from them and sold them to shops. He did painting and decorating for the people in the community. He helped out in a bookshop, two days a week. Throughout all this time, Benjamin created poems. He made contact and then kept in touch with his brothers and sisters, and his reading and writing improved by the day.

He performed his poetry, wherever and whenever: on pavements, in town halls, in community centres and even in churches.

It was political and critical, funny and peculiar.

It was happier and snappier than anything else in town.

Nothing was too insignificant to be included . In his collection of poems, *Talking Turkeys*, he taunts the carnivores to ...

Be nice to yu turkey dis Christmas
Invite dem indoors fe sum greens
Let dem eat cake an let dem partake
In a plate of organic grown beans.

CHAPTER THIRTEEN
Attracting Attention

B ENJAMIN'S GENIUS SEEMED BOUNDLESS. One day, his attention would be on animal rights, the next day it would be pollution.

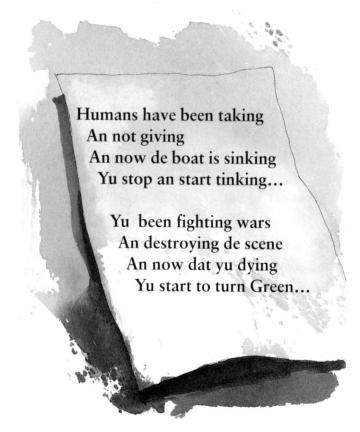

Humans have been taking
An not giving
An now de boat is sinking
Yu stop an start tinking...

Yu been fighting wars
An destroying de scene
An now dat yu dying
Yu start to turn Green...

Wherever he performed the crowds gathered. One Friday night, when Benjamin was performing in the local town hall, he spotted the vicar from his mother's church in the audience.

"Crikey," he muttered, "I'd better leave out the poem with the funny vicar in it. Maybe it wasn't that funny anyway," he said to himself.

But Benjamin got so carried away by the enthusiasm of the audience, he did the 'vicar' poem anyway.

After his performance, Benjamin saw the vicar pushing his way forward through the crowd.

"Mum'll kill me. She's always going on about not doing irreverent jokes about the Reverend."

Benjamin held his breath and waited as the vicar headed straight towards him.

"I read in the papers today," said the vicar, "that there is a poetry competition going on. Can I help you enter it?" Benjamin couldn't believe his ears.

They were still ringing anyway with the loud cheering from the enthusiastic audience. He relaxed his shoulders which he'd scrunched up beneath his warm ears.

"Yessir!! Please. Thank you!" he blurted out and breathed again.

He won the competition. The papers published some of his best poems and suddenly everyone was interested in him. His audience numbers rocketed.

CHAPTER FOURTEEN

Fame at Last

BENJAMIN'S LIFE CHANGED. Thousands of people flocked to hear his poetry.

"I knew it all along," his mother whispered to a friend one night as he performed to a full house in an enormous town hall.

"He's a genius. Just look at all these people clapping and asking for more!"

He was invited to travel to Palestine, Argentina and Uruguay.

He went. Millions flocked to hear his poems. He conquered millions with his verse.

He made them laugh.

He made them cry.

He made them think.

Benjamin was on the move. He was travelling all over the world. This time, not as a little boy lost, but as a brilliantly successful poet.

He had many surprises. Two of the biggest were being asked to be Poet in Residence at both Oxford and Cambridge Universities. Benjamin was chuffed.

His mother was thrilled to share his good times. Benjamin loved seeing her so happy, but sometimes he remembered the sad times.

One day, he asked her how she had managed to put up with all the hardship of those early years and how she'd ever coped with him, with all the trouble he'd caused her.

"I knew you'd make it, Benjamin, because I knew...

> You had a Sonnet
> Under yu bonnet
> And a Novel
> In yu navel."

And they both doubled up laughing.

"Seriously now," she said to Benjamin. "Do you know my proudest moment, son?"

"Tell me," said Benjamin.

"It was the day I saw your picture on the front page of the newspaper, shaking hands with Nelson Mandela, my hero."

"And mine," said Benjamin.

Dere's a Sonnet
Under me bonnet
Dere's a Epic
In me ear
Dere's a Novel
In me navel
Dere's a Classic
Here somewhere.

Dere's a Movie
In me left knee
A long story
In me right
Dere's a shorty
Inbetweeny
It is tickly
In de night.

Dere's a picture
In me ticker
Unmixed riddims
In me heart.
In me texture
Dere's a comma
In me fat chin
Dere is Art.

Dere's an Opera in me bladder
A Ballad's in me wrist
Dere is laughter
In me shoulder
In me guzzard's
A nice twist.

In me dreadlocks
Dere is syntax
A dance kicks
In me bum.
Thru me blood tracks
Dere run true facts
I got limericks
From me Mum.

Documentaries
In me entries
Plays on history
In me folk
Dere's a Trilogy
When I tink of three
On me toey
Dere's a joke.

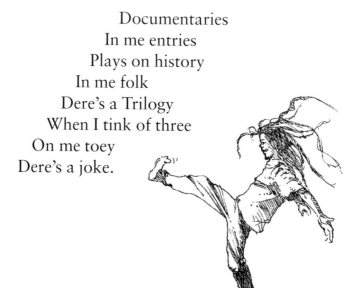